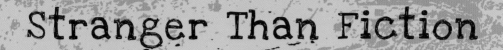

Stranger Than Fiction

D0009110

STUPID CRIMINALS

By Virginia Loh-Hagan

Disclaimer: This series focuses on the strangest of the strange. Have fun reading about strange people and things! But please do not try any of the antics in this book. Be safe and smart!

45th Parallel Press

Published in the United States of America by Cherry Lake Publishing
Ann Arbor, Michigan
www.cherrylakepublishing.com

Reading Adviser: Marla Conn MS, Ed., Literacy specialist, Read-Ability, Inc.
Book Designer: Melinda Millward

Photo Credits: © SeanShot/iStockphoto, cover, 7; © Kimber Rey Solana/Shutterstock.com, 1; © Corepics VOF/Shutterstock.com, 5; © SunyawitPhoto/Shutterstock.com, 6; © Sheila Fitzgerald/Shutterstock.com, 8; © RichLegg/iStockphoto, 9; © Andreas Gradin/Shutterstock.com, 10; © izusek/iStockphoto, 11; © alexrvan/iStockphoto, 12; © prill/Thinkstock, 14; © Jane Rahman, www.flickr.com/buenosaurus/ Getty Images, 15; © ktylr/iStockphoto, 16; © Rob Bayer/Shutterstock.com, 17; © J_K/Shutterstock.com, 18; © Anan Kaewkhammul/Shutterstock.com, 19; © Finnphotog/iStockphoto, 20; © Klearchos Kapoutsis/http://www.flickr.com/ CC-BY-2.0, 22; © Galyna Andrushko/Shutterstock.com, 23; © El Nariz/Shutterstock.com, 24; © dundanim/iStockphoto, 25; © Melinda Millward, 26; © file404/Shutterstock.com, 27; © nikamo/Shutterstock.com, 28; © Chayantorn Tongmorn/Shutterstock.com, 30; © SEASTOCK/Shutterstock.com, 31

Graphic Element Credits: ©saki80/Shutterstock.com, back cover, front cover, multiple interior pages; ©queezz/Shutterstock.com, back cover, front cover, multiple interior pages; ©Ursa Major/Shutterstock.com, front cover, multiple interior pages; ©Zilu8/Shutterstock.com, multiple interior pages

45th Parallel Press is an imprint of Cherry Lake Publishing.

Library of Congress Cataloging-in-Publication Data has been filed and is available at catalog.loc.gov

Printed in the United States of America
Corporate Graphics

About the Author

Dr. Virginia Loh-Hagan is an author, university professor, former classroom teacher, and curriculum designer. Her strangest crime is letting her dogs get away with murder. She lives in San Diego with her very tall husband and very naughty dogs. To learn more about her, visit www.virginialoh.com.

Table of Contents

Introduction

Some people break laws. They don't follow rules. They commit **crimes**. They're criminals. Many criminals get caught. Police officers **arrest** them. Arrest means to take someone to jail.

There are smart criminals. And there are stupid criminals. Stupid criminals do stupid crimes. They don't think. They make mistakes. They get caught.

Some stupid criminals are strange. But other criminals are really strange. Some criminals do strange crimes. They get caught in strange ways. They're so strange that they're hard to believe. They sound like fiction. But these stories are all true!

Laws are a system of rules.

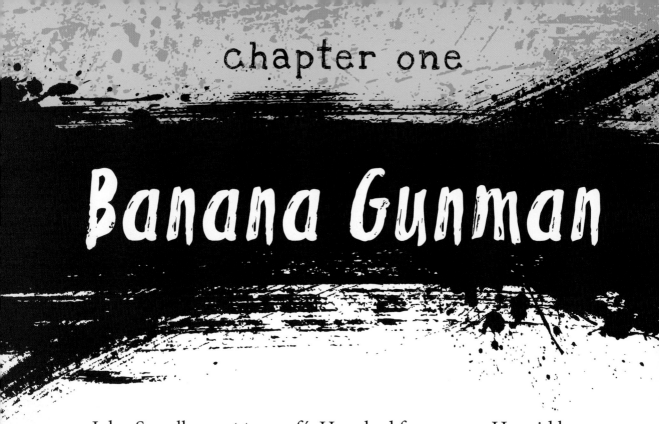

chapter one

Banana Gunman

John Szwalla went to a café. He asked for money. He said he had a gun. He said it was under his shirt. He was 17 years old.

The café owner and a customer acted. They held Szwalla down. They called the cops. They found out Szwalla didn't have a gun. His gun was a banana.

Szwalla waited for the cops. He got hungry. He ate his banana. Cops joked. They said he was "destroying **evidence.**" Evidence is proof. Cops took pictures of the banana peel.

Hiding a weapon is against the law.

Szwalla was charged with **attempted armed** robbery. Attempt means to try. Armed means having a weapon.

chapter two

Penny Stealer

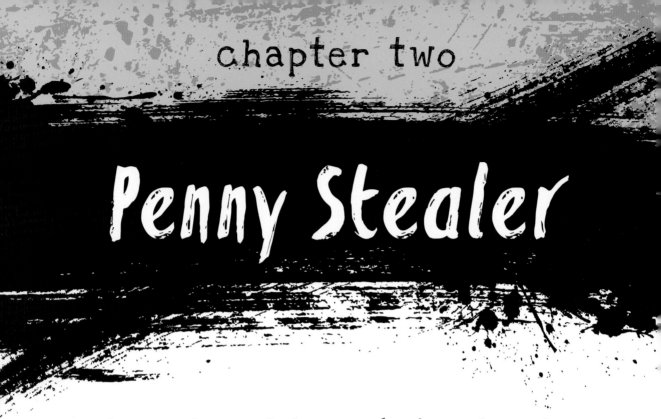

Robert Napolitan worked as a **mechanic**. Mechanics fix machines. He stole a steel **drum** from work. A drum is a container. It had 300,000 pennies in it. He went to work late. He said he was working on a car. He put the drum on a hand truck. He rolled it to his truck. He left tracks through the dust. He left a trail of pennies. He marked his path. He was also caught on camera.

Cops searched his truck. They found pennies under seats. They found pennies under floor mats. Napolitan **confessed**. Confess means to admit fault. He went to jail.

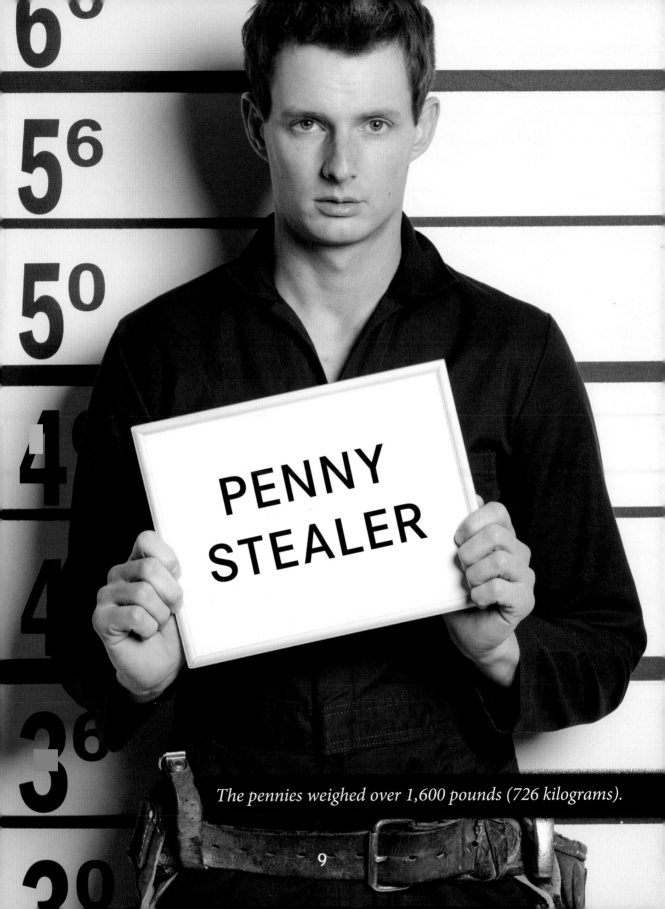

PENNY STEALER

The pennies weighed over 1,600 pounds (726 kilograms).

chapter three

Animal Smugglers

Sharon Naismith was on a plane. She traveled from Australia. She landed in Singapore. Airport officials heard flipping sounds. The sounds came from her waist. Naismith wore an apron. The apron was under her skirt. It was filled with bags of fish. It had 51 fish. The fish were special.

Naismith was caught. She **smuggled**. This means she tried to sneak something in. She was **sentenced**. Sentenced means to punish. She did nine months of community service.

Smuggling wildlife is against the law.

Naismith said her crime was loving fish. She has many fish tanks. Officials found **illegal** fish in her house. Illegal means against the law.

There are other fish lovers. One guy robbed stores. He was armed. He had a large knife. He needed money. He used the money for fish. He built a fancy fish tank. He collected fancy fish. His lawyer said his love of fish was "stupid." He was jailed for 18 months.

Fish aren't the only smuggled animals. There was a woman in Sweden. She tried to smuggle 75 live snakes. She hid them in her bra. She also had six lizards. She hid them under her shirt. She wanted to start a reptile farm. She scratched her chest. Airport officials thought it was strange. They arrested her.

Smuggling hurts the animals.

Explained by Science

People have fingers. Fingers leave prints on things. Fingerprints are impressions. They have ridges. Ridges have pores. Pores are attached to sweat glands under the skin. This sweat is how people leave prints. Prints are left on surfaces. They identify people. Everyone has a different fingerprint. They're part of biometrics. This is a science. It uses people's physical traits to identify them. Forensic scientists study crime scenes. They collect fingerprints. Then, they study fingerprints. They count ridges. They look at folds. They look at loops. They look at whorls. They look at arches. They compare one set of fingerprints to another. They verify matches. They use fingerprints to identify criminals. So, smart criminals wear gloves.

chapter four

Marker Bandits

Joey Miller and Matthew McNelly tried to rob a house. They wore hooded sweatshirts. They drew on their faces. They used black permanent markers. They drew beards. They drew mustaches. They couldn't erase their disguises afterwards. This made them easy to find. They tried to get away. They drove a big white car.

Cops pulled them over. They said guilt was written all over their faces. A cop said, "I've never heard of coloring your face with a permanent marker. … It's a little weird."

Smart criminals wear ski masks or stockings over their head.

Miller and McNelly were released. There wasn't enough proof. They didn't have weapons. No one got hurt. But everyone laughed at them.

chapter five

Air Horn Guy

John Nuggent bothered people. He blasted an air horn. He did this early in the morning. He did this for six weeks. He ran away before cops came.

Cops caught him at 4:00 a.m. on a Sunday. They followed the sound. They found a car. They pulled over the driver. They found Nuggent. They found air horn gear.

Nuggent confessed. He was mad at someone. He wanted to get even. He wanted to wake people up. People were mad. They complained. They said they

Disturbing the peace is a crime.

were victims. They made a **citizens**' arrest. This means regular people can charge a criminal.

chapter six

Tiger Mother

Trisha Meyer lived in Texas. She called officials. She asked about getting a **permit** to keep tigers. Permits give someone permission. Several days later, she rented a van. She had three tiger cubs. She kept them in her house. She treated them like house cats. She let them roam outside her house. She didn't restrain them. Her fence was only 4 feet (1.2 meters) high.

The tigers didn't attack. But neighbors were scared. They complained. They reported the tigers.

Cops came. They saw tiger cubs eating raw chicken. They found other animals. They found an adult tiger. They found eight

There are laws about keeping wild animals.

monkeys. They found a fox. They found a skunk.

Meyer didn't have all her permits. Cops arrested her. They took the animals away.

Meyer has a teenage daughter. Cops thought the animals could've hurt the teenager. Meyer confessed. She said the tigers were old enough to kill. She said the monkeys could be mean.

An official said, "Having wildlife inside your home or even in your yard is dangerous. Wildlife can pose a threat to anyone in the house, especially if it isn't restrained."

Meyer fled to Nevada. She was charged with stealing animals. She was charged with putting a child in danger.

Animals are taken to an animal control agency.

20

Spotlight Biography

Laura Spaulding lived in Missouri. She was a cop. She saw many crime scenes. Crimes can be messy. One crime was a home shooting. The house owner wanted her house to be cleaned. Spaulding felt bad for the owner. She helped clean the mess. This inspired her. Now, she lives in Florida. She's a crime scene cleaner. Her company is called Spaulding Decon. She cleans up messes. She cleans blood. She cleans poisons. She wears a protective suit. She wears tall boots. She wears rubber gloves. She said, "We are covered from head to toe." She uses powerful cleaners. She uses special vacuums. She helps people.

chapter seven

Bear Suit Dude

There's a strange criminal in Alaska. A man wore a bear suit. The suit looked real. It had a head. It had a body.

The man went to a river. This is where bears catch food. Bears hunt for salmon. The man bothered the bears. He jumped up and down. He got close to the bear cubs. Then, he got in his car. He drove away. He kept his bear suit on.

No one knows why he did this. An official said, "This is not the first time we've encountered a man in a bear suit."

Fish and game departments are in charge of the state's wildlife.

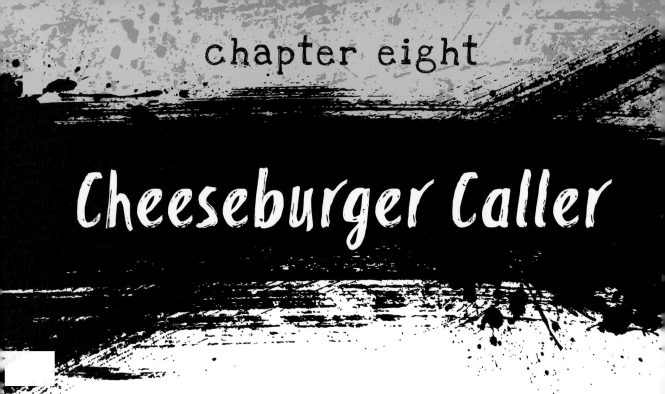

chapter eight

Cheeseburger Caller

Gregory Jackson Sr. lives in Indiana. He was really hungry. He wanted a cheeseburger. He called 911. He demanded a cop bring him a cheeseburger. He called nine times. He did this in 90 minutes.

The **dispatcher** said, "We don't take cheeseburger orders." Dispatchers handle phone calls. They sent cops to his house. They thought the calls were strange. Jackson was on the phone when the cops came.

Cops arrested him. They caught him on past charges. Jackson had a **warrant** for his arrest. Warrants are orders. Jackson

24

911 is for emergency calls only.

didn't get a cheeseburger. He got a peanut butter and jelly sandwich. He ate it in jail.

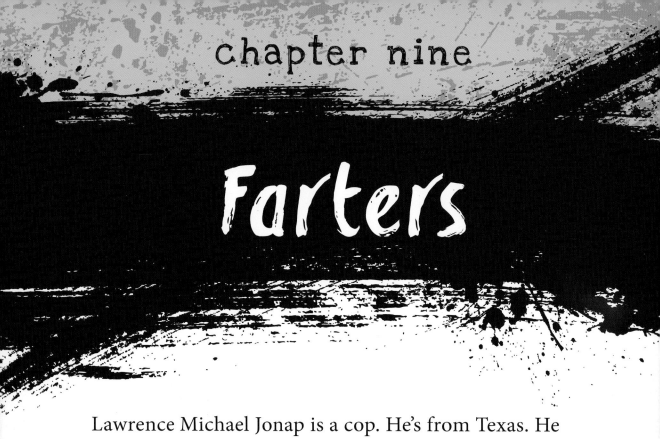

chapter nine

Farters

Lawrence Michael Jonap is a cop. He's from Texas. He got mad at Donald Varner. Varner is a dispatcher.

Jonap walked by Varner. He kicked him in the back. He laughed. Varner reported him. Jonap didn't stop. He bullied Varner the next day. He threw a notebook at him. He flicked his ear. Then, he farted in his face.

He was charged with **assault** with injury. Assault means attack. It's when someone tries to hurt another person. He wasn't charged with **battery**. Battery means

Assault with injury could lead to a year in jail and $4,000 in fines.

making harmful contact. Farting on someone is not battery.
Farting on someone is assault.

Jose Cruz also got busted for farting. He was pulled over. He drove without headlights. He smelled like alcohol. He was taken to a police station.

He was being fingerprinted. He moved near a cop. He lifted his leg. He farted on the cop. He fanned his fart. He pushed it toward the cop. The cop said the fart smelled. He was offended.

Cruz was arrested. He confessed to farting many times. But he denied aiming his fart. He said he had an upset stomach. He said the cop wouldn't let him use the bathroom. He said, "I couldn't hold it no more."

Cops test to see if people are drunk or not.

Try This!

- Read your local crime report. This can be found in the local newspaper or online. What is the most common crime? Which crime seems the silliest? Which crimes seem the most serious?

- Make a list of school rules. Think about each rule. List the punishment for breaking each rule.

- Talk to a police officer. Ask what it's like to catch criminals. Ask how the police officer keeps law and order.

- Talk to a judge. Ask what it's like to sentence criminals.

- Research your local jail. Find out where it is. Find out what types of criminals are there.

- Don't break any laws! Stay out of trouble!

chapter ten

Mr. Flusher

Ralph Curry lived in an apartment building. **Maintenance** didn't respond to his calls. Maintenance are people who take care of buildings. Curry got mad.

He cooked a bag of potatoes. He shoved them down his toilet. He clogged up his toilet. Water came out. His bathroom flooded. He called maintenance again. Nobody responded. Curry pulled a fire alarm. Everyone had to leave the building. Firefighters found the clogged toilet.

Curry was arrested. He "caused public alarm." He caused 12 families to be out

Making false alarms is against the law.

in the cold. This could have harmed them. He wasted the firemen's time. This put the public at risk. And all for a clogged toilet.

Consider This!

Take a Position! Minors are people under 18 years old. Some minors commit serious crimes. Do you think minors should be charged as adults? Argue your point with reasons and evidence.

Say What? Think about the last time you broke a rule. This is like committing a crime. Explain what you did. Explain the consequences. Consequences are punishments.

Think About It! Committing a crime is pretty stupid. The benefits must be better than the risks. Why do people commit crimes? Would you take the risks?

Learn More!

- MacDonald, Fiona, and David Antram (illustrator). *You Wouldn't Want to Meet a Body Snatcher! Criminals and Murderers You'd Rather Avoid*. New York: Franklin Watts, 2009.
- National Geographic and Tom Nick Cocotos (illustrator). *Weird but True! Stupid Criminals: 150 Brainless Baddies Busted, Plus Wacky Facts*. Washington, DC: National Geographic Children's Books, 2012.

Glossary

armed (AHRMD) having weapons

arrest (uh-REST) to take someone to jail

assault (uh-SAWLT) an attack intended to hurt another person

attempted (uh-TEMPT-id) tried

battery (BAT-ur-ee) an attack that makes harmful contact

citizens (SIT-ih-zuhnz) people belonging to a country

confessed (kuhn-FESD) admitted fault

crimes (KRYMZ) acts that break the law

dispatcher (DIS-pach-ur) an emergency call coordinator

drum (DRUHM) a container

evidence (EV-ih-duhns) proof

illegal (ih-LEE-guhl) against the law

maintenance (MAYN-tuh-nuhns) staff that takes care of buildings

mechanic (muh-KAN-ik) someone who fixes machines like cars

permit (PUR-mit) a document giving official permission

sentenced (SEN-tuhnsd) punished

smuggled (SMUHG-uhld) snuck something in

warrant (WOR-uhnt) an order

Index